# PROMISES

*God's Word ...*
*Now and Forever*

Barbour Books, Westwood, New Jersey

© 1991 by Barbour and Company, Inc.

All Scripture is from the King James Version of the Bible

Published by **Barbour and Company, Inc., P.O. Box 1219, Westwood, New Jersey 07675.**

Typesetting by Typetronix, Inc., Cape Coral, Florida

ISBN 1-55748-254-3

Printed in the United States of America

1  2  3  4  5/ 96  95  94  93  92  91

*If* instead of a gem, or even a flower, we could cast the gift of a lovely thought into the heart of a friend, that would be giving as the angels give.

GEORGE MacDONALD

For God so loved the world, that he gave his only begotten Son, that whosoever believeth in him should not perish, but have everlasting life.

*John 3:16*

I am come a light into the world, that whosoever believeth on me should not abide in darkness. *John 12:46*

And Jesus said unto them, I am the bread of life: he that cometh to me shall never hunger; and he that believeth on me shall never thirst.    *John 6:35*

And all thy children shall be taught of the LORD; and great shall be the peace of thy children.   *Isaiah 54:13*

Verily I say unto you, Whosoever shall not receive the kingdom of God as a little child, he shall not enter therein. And he took them up in his arms, put his hands upon them, and blessed them. *Mark 10:14–16*

L̤o, children are an heritage of the
LORD: and the fruit of the womb is his
reward.                     *Psalm 127:3*

Children's children are the crown of old men; and the glory of children are their fathers.     *Proverbs 17:6*

God is our refuge and strength, a very present help in trouble.

*Psalm 46:1*

Come unto me, all ye that labour and are heavy laden, and I will give you rest. *Matthew 11:28*

Wait on the LORD: be of good
courage, and he shall strengthen
thine heart: wait, I say, on the LORD.

*Psalm 27:14*

The LORD is good, a strong hold in the day of trouble; and he knoweth them that trust in him.     *Nahum 1:7*

Let your conversation be without covetousness; and be content with such things as ye have: for he hath said, I will never leave thee, nor forsake thee.        *Hebrews 13:5*

Rejoice evermore. Pray without ceasing. In every thing give thanks: for this is the will of God in Christ Jesus concerning you.   *1 Thessalonians 5:16-18*

Let us not be desirous of vain glory, provoking one another, envying one another. *Galatians 5:26*

Peace I leave with you, my peace I give unto you: not as the world giveth, give I unto you. Let not your heart be troubled, neither let it be afraid.

*John 14:27*

...Fear not: for they that be with us
are more than they that be with them.
*2 Kings 6:16*

He giveth power to the faint; and to them that have no might he increaseth strength. *Isaiah 40:29*

I can do all things through Christ which strengtheneth me.

*Philippians 4:12,13*

For God hath not given us the spirit of fear; but of power, and of love, and of a sound mind.  *2 Timothy 1:7*

Verily, verily, I say unto you, He that believeth on me hath everlasting life.       *John  6:47*

In my Father's house are many mansions: if it were not so, I would have told you. I go to prepare a place for you. *John 14:2*

My sheep hear my voice, and I know them, and they follow me: And I give unto them eternal life; and they shall never perish, neither shall any man pluck them out of my hand.

*John 10:27,28*

Jesus said unto her, I am the resurrection, and the life: he that believeth in me, though he were dead, yet shall he live: And whosoever liveth and believeth in me shall never die.

*John 11:25, 26*

Now faith is the substance of things hoped for, the evidence of things not seen.          *Hebrews 11:1*

I have fought a good fight, I have finished my course, I have kept the faith. *2 Timothy 4:7*

... Let us run with patience the race that is set before us, Looking unto Jesus the author and finisher of our faith; who for the joy that was set before him endured the cross, despising the shame, and is set down at the right hand of the throne of God.

*Hebrews 12:1,2*

And now, little children, abide in him; that, when he shall appear, we may have confidence, and not be ashamed before him at his coming.

*1 John 2:28*

$A$nd fear not them which kill the body, but are not able to kill the soul .... *Matthew 10:28*

... Behold, the fear of the Lord, that is wisdom; and to depart from evil is understanding. *Job 28:28*

Fear not, little flock; for it is your Father's good pleasure to give you the kingdom. *Luke 12:32*

The LORD is my light and my salvation; whom shall I fear? the LORD is the strength of my life; of whom shall I be afraid?

Though an host should encamp against me, my heart shall not fear: though war should rise against me, in this will I be confident.

*Psalm 27:1,3*

35

Therefore take no thought, saying, What shall we eat? or, What shall we drink? or, Wherewithal shall we be clothed? ... for your heavenly Father knoweth that ye have need of all these things.     *Matthew 6:31,32*

He causeth the grass to grow for the cattle, and herb for the service of man: that he may bring forth food out of the earth.       *Psalm 104:14*

But my God shall supply all your need according to his riches in glory by Christ Jesus.     *Philippians 4:19*

Be careful for nothing; but in every thing by prayer and supplication with thanksgiving let your requests be made known unto God. And the peace of God, which passeth all understanding, shall keep your hearts and minds through Christ Jesus. *Philippians 4:6,7*

39

Bunt I say unto you, Love your en-
emies, bless them that curse you, do
good to them that hate you, and pray
for them which despitefully use you,
and persecute you.      *Matthew 5:44*

Judge not, and ye shall not be judged: condemn not, and ye shall not be condemned: forgive, and ye shall be forgiven. *Luke 6:37*

If we confess our sins, he is faithful and just to forgive us our sins, and to cleanse us from all unrighteousness.

*1 John 1:9*

As far as the east is from the west, so far hath he removed our transgressions from us. *Psalm 103:12*

I am the vine, ye are the branches:
He that abideth in me, and I in him,
the same bringeth forth much fruit:
for without me ye can do nothing.

*John 15:5*

And I myself also am persuaded of you, my brethren, that ye also are full of goodness, filled with all knowledge, able also to admonish one another.

*Romans 15:14*

For the fruit of the Spirit is in all goodness and righteousness and truth.

*Ephesians 5:9*

But the fruit of the Spirit is love, joy, peace, longsuffering, gentleness, goodness, faith, meekness, temperance: against such there is no law.

*Galatians 5:22,23*

Let the words of my mouth, and the meditation of my heart, be acceptable in thy sight, O Lord, my strength, and my redeemer. *Psalm 19:14*

For by thy words thou shalt be justified, and by thy words thou shalt be condemned.          *Matthew 12:37*

Whoso keepeth his mouth and his tongue keepeth his soul from troubles.

*Proverbs 21:23*

Set a watch, O Lord, before my mouth; keep the door of my lips.

*Psalm 141:3*

And now, brethren, I commend you to God, and to the word of his grace, which is able to build you up, and to give you an inheritance among all them which are sanctified.

*Acts 20:32*

And this I pray, that your love may abound yet more and more in knowledge and in all judgment.

*Philippians 1:9*

But the path of the just is as the shining light, that shineth more and more unto the perfect day.

*Proverbs 4:18*

I press toward the mark for the prize of the high calling of God in Christ Jesus.           *Philippians 3:14*

I will instruct thee and teach thee in the way which thou shalt go: I will guide thee with mine eye.

*Psalm 32:8*

The steps of a good man are ordered by the LORD: and he delighteth in his way. *Psalm 37:23*

For this God is our God for ever and ever: he will be our guide even unto death. *Psalm 48:14*

Trust in the Lord with all thine heart;
and lean not unto thine own understanding. In all thy ways acknowl-
edge him, and he shall direct thy
paths.                    *Proverbs 3:5,6*

Thou art my hiding place; thou shalt preserve me from trouble; thou shalt compass me about with songs of deliverance.                 *Psalm 32:7*

These things I have spoken unto you, that in me ye might have peace. In the world ye shall have tribulation: but be of good cheer; I have overcome the world. *John 16:33*

Many are the afflictions of the righteous: but the Lord delivereth him out of them all.                    *Psalm 34:19*

For I reckon that the sufferings of this present time are not worthy to be compared with the glory which shall be revealed in us.

*Romans 8:18*

Withhold not good from them to whom it is due, when it is in the power of thine hand to do it.

*Proverbs 3:27*

B ut thou shalt have a perfect and just weight, a perfect and just measure shalt thou have: that thy days may be lengthened in the land which the LORD thy God giveth thee.

*Deuteronomy 25:15*

Buy the truth, and sell it not; also wisdom, and instruction, and understanding. *Proverbs 23:23*

By mercy and truth iniquity is purged:
and by the fear of the Lord men depart
from evil. *Proverbs 16:6*

And every man that hath this hope
in him purifieth himself, even as he
is pure.                    *1 John 3:3*

Behold, the eye of the Lord is upon them that fear him, upon them that hope in his mercy.     *Psalm 33:18*

F or thou art my hope, O Lord GOD:
thou art my trust from my youth.

*Psalm 71:5*

It is good that a man should both hope and quietly wait for the salvation of the Lord. *Lamentations 3:26*

Use hospitality one to another without grudging. As every man hath received the gift, even so minister the same one to another, as good stewards of the manifold grace of God.

*1 Peter 4:9,10*

For I was an hungred, and ye gave me meat: I was thirsty, and ye gave me drink: I was a stranger, and ye took me in: Naked, and ye clothed me: I was sick, and ye visited me: I was in prison, and ye came unto me.

*Matthew 25:35,36*

B e not forgetful to entertain strangers: for thereby some have entertained angels unawares. *Hebrews 13:2*

For whosoever shall give you a cup
of water to drink in my name, because ye belong to Christ, verily I
say unto you, he shall not lose his
reward.                    *Mark 9:41*

Whosoever therefore shall humble himself as this little child, the same is greatest in the kingdom of heaven.

*Matthew 18:4*

Better it is to be of an humble spirit with the lowly, than to divide the spoil with the proud.

*Proverbs 16:19*

L ORD, thou hast heard the desire of the humble: thou wilt prepare their heart, thou wilt cause thine ear to hear. *Psalm 10:17*

Let another man praise thee, and not thine own mouth; a stranger, and not thine own lips.     *Proverbs 27:2*

For where envying and strife is, there is confusion and every evil work.

*James 3:16*

Rest in the LORD, and wait patiently
for him: fret not thyself because of
him who prospereth in his way.

*Psalm 37:7*

A sound heart is the life of the flesh: but envy the rottenness of the bones. *Proverbs 14:30*

Charity suffereth long, and is kind;
charity envieth not; charity vaunteth
not itself, is not puffed up.

*1 Corinthians 13:4*

For God giveth to a man that is good in his sight wisdom, and knowledge, and joy.              *Ecclesiastes 2:26*

For ye shall go out with joy, and be led forth with peace: the mountains and the hills shall break forth before you into singing, and all the trees of the field shall clap their hands.      *Isaiah 55:12*

Blessed is the people that know the joyful sound: they shall walk, O LORD, in the light of thy countenance. In thy name shall they rejoice all the day: and in thy righteousness shall they be exalted. *Psalm 89:15,16*

... I will see you again, and your heart shall rejoice, and your joy no man taketh from you.                    *John 16:22*

Then shalt thou call, and the LORD shall answer; thou shalt cry, and he shall say, Here I am ....          *Isaiah 58:9*

And he said, My presence shall go with thee, and I will give thee rest.

*Exodus 33:14*

And, behold, I am with thee, and will keep thee in all places whither thou goest, and will bring thee again into this land; for I will not leave thee, until I have done that which I have spoken to thee of. *Genesis 28:15*

I will not leave you comfortless: I will come to you.          *John 14:18*

Cast me not off in the time of old age;
forsake me not when my strength faileth.

*Psalm 71:9*

LORD, make me to know mine end, and the measure of my days, what it is; that I may know how frail I am.

Behold, thou hast made my days as an handbreadth; and mine age is as nothing before thee ....     *Psalm 39:4,5*

The glory of young men is their strength: and the beauty of old men is the gray head.                    *Proverbs 20:29*

Ye shall walk in all the ways which the
LORD your God hath commanded you,
that ye may live, and that it may be well
with you, and that ye may prolong your
days in the land which ye shall possess.

*Deuteronomy 5:33*

Therefore shall a man leave his father and his mother, and shall cleave unto his wife: and they shall be one flesh.

*Genesis 2:24*

Husbands, love your wives, even as Christ also loved the church, and gave himself for it. *Ephesians 5:25*

Whoso findeth a wife findeth a good
thing, and obtaineth favour of the Lord.
*Proverbs 18:22*

Nevertheless let every one of you in particular so love his wife even as himself; and the wife see that she reverence her husband. *Ephesians 5:33*

The Lord is gracious, and full of compassion; slow to anger, and of great mercy. The Lord is good to all: and his tender mercies are over all his works.

*Psalm 145:8,9*

100

Yet thou in thy manifold mercies forsookest
them not in the wilderness.     *Nehemiah 9:19*

And therefore will the LORD wait, that he may be gracious unto you, and therefore will he be exalted, that he may have mercy upon you: for the LORD is a God of judgment: blessed are all they that wait for him. *Isaiah 30:18*

But the mercy of the LORD is from everlasting to everlasting upon them that fear him, and his righteousness unto children's children.

*Psalm 103:17*

Labour not to be rich: cease from thine own wisdom. Wilt thou set thine eyes upon that which is not? for riches certainly make themselves wings; they fly away as an eagle toward heaven.

*Proverbs 23:4,5*

The silver is mine, and the gold is mine, saith the Lord of hosts. *Haggai 2:8*

Honour the Lord with thy substance, and with the firstfruits of all thine increase: So shall thy barns be filled with plenty, and thy presses shall burst out with new wine.     *Proverbs 3:9,10*

$\text{B}$etter is little with the fear of the LORD than great treasure and trouble therewith.  *Proverbs 15:16*

And we know that all things work together for good to them that love God, to them who are the called according to his purpose.    *Romans 8:28*

If ye keep my commandments, ye shall abide in my love; even as I have kept my Father's commandments, and abide in his love. *John 15:10*

Those things, which ye have both learned, and received, and heard, and seen in me, do: and the God of peace shall be with you. *Philippians 4:9*

And the world passeth away, and the lust thereof: but he that doeth the will of God abideth for ever.      *1 John 2:17*

But he that shall endure unto the end, the same shall be saved.

*Matthew 24:13*

And not only so, but we glory in tribulations also: knowing that tribulation worketh patience, and patience, experience: and experience, hope.

*Romans 5:3,4*

113

For ye have need of patience, that, after ye have done the will of God, ye might receive the promise.

*Hebrews 10:36*

Let us hold fast the profession of our faith without wavering; for he is faithful that promised. *Hebrews 10:23*

And the peace of God, which passeth
all understanding, shall keep your hearts
and minds through Christ Jesus.

*Philippians 4:7*

M ark the perfect man, and behold the upright: for the end of that man is peace. *Psalm 37:37*

For unto us a child is born, unto us a son is given: and the government shall be upon his shoulder: and his name shall be called Wonderful, Counsellor, The mighty God, The everlasting Father, The Prince of Peace. *Isaiah 9:6*

Thou wilt keep him in perfect peace,
whose mind is stayed on thee: because
he trusteth in thee. *Isaiah 26:3*

Ask, and it shall be given you; seek, and ye shall find; knock, and it shall be opened unto you: For every one that asketh receiveth; and he that seeketh findeth; and to him that knocketh it shall be opened.      *Matthew 7:7,8*

Let us therefore come boldly unto the throne of grace, that we may obtain mercy, and find grace to help in time of need. *Hebrews 4:16*

And all things, whatsoever ye shall ask in prayer, believing, ye shall receive.

*Matthew 21:22*

Rejoice evermore. Pray without ceasing. In every thing give thanks: for this is the will of God in Christ Jesus concerning you.

*1 Thessalonians 5:16–18*

123

Pride goeth before destruction, and an haughty spirit before a fall.

*Proverbs 16:18*

Woe unto them that are wise in their own eyes, and prudent in their own sight!                    *Isaiah 5:21*

And whosoever shall exalt himself shall be abased; and he that shall humble himself shall be exalted.

*Matthew 23:12*

Though the Lord be high, yet hath he respect unto the lowly: but the proud he knoweth afar off.          *Psalm 138:6*

127

... The time is fulfilled, and the kingdom of God is at hand: repent ye, and believe the gospel.                                    *Mark 1:15*

He healeth the broken in heart, and bindeth up their wounds. *Psalm 147:3*

I say unto you, that likewise joy shall be in heaven over one sinner that repenteth, more than over ninety and nine just persons, which need no repentance.

*Luke 15:7*

The Lord is not slack concerning his promise, as some men count slackness; but is longsuffering to us-ward, not willing that any should perish, but that all should come to repentance.

*2 Peter 3:9*

Blessed are they which do hunger and thirst after righteousness: for they shall be filled. *Matthew 5:6*

He that spared not his own Son, but delivered him up for us all, how shall he not with him also freely give us all things?                    *Romans 8:32*

But seek ye first the kingdom of God, and his righteousness; and all these things shall be added unto you.

*Matthew 6:33*

Surely goodness and mercy shall follow me all the days of my life: and I will dwell in the house of the LORD for ever.

*Psalm 23:6*

Jesus answered and said unto him, Verily, verily, I say unto thee, Except a man be born again, he cannot see the kingdom of God. *John 3:3*

...And if any man sin, we have an advocate with the Father, Jesus Christ the righteous: And he is the propitiation for our sins: and not for ours only, but also for the sins of the whole world.

*1 John 2:1,2*

For by grace are ye saved through faith; and that not of yourselves: it is the gift of God: Not of works, lest any man should boast. *Ephesians 2:8,9*

Jesus saith unto him, I am the way, the truth, and the life: no man cometh unto the Father, but by me.          *John 14:6*

139

Therefore if any man be in Christ, he is a new creature: old things are passed away; behold, all things are become new. *2 Corinthians 5:17*

What shall we say then? Shall we continue in sin, that grace may abound? God forbid. How shall we, that are dead to sin, live any longer therein?

*Romans 6:1,2*

For the wages of sin is death; but the gift of God is eternal life through Jesus Christ our Lord.          *Romans 6:23*

For sin shall not have dominion over you: for ye are not under the law, but under grace. *Romans 6:14*

 By humility and the fear of the LORD
are riches, and honour, and life.

*Proverbs 22:4*

And also that every man should eat and drink, and enjoy the good of all his labour, it is the gift of God.

*Ecclesiastes 3:13*

The Lord maketh poor, and maketh rich: he bringeth low, and lifteth up.

*1 Samuel 2:7*

For thou shalt eat the labour of thine hands: happy shalt thou be, and it shall be well with thee. *Psalm 128:2*

Our fathers trusted in thee: they trusted,
and thou didst deliver them.

*Psalm 22:4*

They that trust in the LORD shall be as
mount Zion, which cannot be removed,
but abideth for ever.          *Psalm 125:1*

It is better to trust in the Lord than to put confidence in man. It is better to trust in the Lord than to put confidence in princes. *Psalm 118:8,9*

150

Thou wilt keep him in perfect peace, whose mind is stayed on thee: because he trusteth in thee. Trust ye in the Lord for ever: for in the Lord JEHOVAH is everlasting strength.     *Isaiah 26:3,4*

If any of you lack wisdom, let him ask of God, that giveth to all men liberally, and upbraideth not; and it shall be given him. *James 1:5*

Happy is the man that findeth wisdom, and the man that getteth understanding. For the merchandise of it is better than the merchandise of silver, and the gain thereof than fine gold.

*Proverbs 3:13,14*

153

But the wisdom that is from above is first pure, then peaceable, gentle, and easy to be intreated, full of mercy and good fruits, without partiality, and without hypocrisy.                    *James 3:17*

The fear of the Lord is the beginning of wisdom: a good understanding have all they that do his commandments: his praise endureth for ever.

*Psalm 111:10*

Thy word is a lamp unto my feet, and
a light unto my path.       *Psalm 119:105*

For the word of God is quick, and power-ful, and sharper than any two-edged sword, piercing even to the dividing asunder of soul and spirit, and of the joints and mar-row, and is a discerner of the thoughts and intents of the heart. *Hebrews 4:12*

157

So then faith cometh by hearing, and hearing by the word of God.

*Romans 10:17*

Blessed is he that readeth, and they that hear the words of this prophecy, and keep those things which are written therein: for the time is at hand.

*Revelation 1:3*